MARCELLA

Dedicated to the real Marcella, who lives in New Zealand, beside the Tasman Sea.

Coco was lost at the beach. She was tired and hungry, and she knew she had to find something to eat.

Then she saw a light outside a house. She could smell a dinner cooking. Although she was frightened, she sat quietly at the edge of the courtyard, where the light became night.

Carol and Ivan lived in the house. Carol looked out the window over the courtyard. "Look," she said, "there's a cat on the fence."

Carol and Ivan felt sorry for her. They could see she was a stray. They left her some food.

Coco learned to visit the courtyard every night. Carol noticed that Coco's stomach was becoming very round.

5

Then one day Coco went to a special hideaway. She made herself comfortable and lay down to wait.

Carol and Ivan called for her in the evenings. They had grown used to her company. But Coco did not come. Where was she?

"Maybe she has gone off to have her babies," said Carol.

Then one morning, about ten days later, Ivan saw a tiny black and white kitten all alone on the lawn. He picked it up and ran inside to Carol.

"You were right," he said. "Coco has had a kitten!"

Then they heard a meow. There was Coco with five more kittens.

Coco led her family inside. They all snuggled up on a rug and Coco fed her kittens. They liked their new home.

9

One kitten seemed more adventurous than the rest, always crawling away from the others and wandering around the room.

Ivan named this kitten Marco Polo, after the great Italian explorer. However, a few days later, Carol decided Marco Polo was a girl, so they renamed her Marcella.

Ivan and Carol gradually realized that Marcella was different from all the rest of the kittens. She became upset if they picked her up. She waved her legs around, looking for the ground.

She was afraid to jump off the couch.
Instead, she would always lower herself slowly down
the front of the couch, paw by paw. When she
walked, she put her feet out in front of her slowly
and carefully.

She didn't play with leaves or string, or pounce on
her mother's tail with the other kittens.

As the kittens grew up, friends of Carol and Ivan came and chose among them, taking them away to new homes.

But Carol and Ivan kept Marcella. She had become special to them when they realized she was blind.

"Blind cats adapt well," said the local vet. "Do you live near a busy road?"

Carol and Ivan explained that they lived near a beach, away from traffic.

"Then she will be fine," said the vet.

And she was.

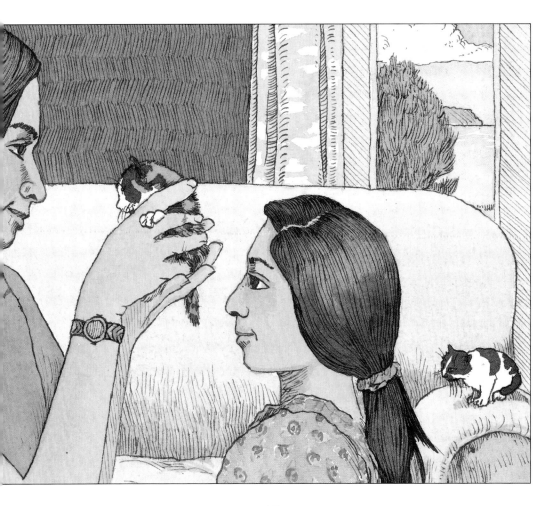

Marcella has grown into a beautiful big cat.

She cannot catch mice like her mother, Coco. She cannot climb trees, and she never tunnels into long grass to hunt for insects. She does not chase string or leaves, or stalk birds.

But in her own special way she does much more.

She has her own hideaway, where she runs when she is frightened. She has her own ramp to help her climb out of the house to the courtyard.

She listens to sounds, holding her head up and waving it from side to side.

Her whiskers tell her if the door is open wide enough for her to run through.

19

She even climbs up the ladder into Ivan's office,
where she nips his ankles while he writes.

Carol and Ivan love her, and she loves them.

21

Every night, when she thinks
Carol and Ivan are asleep,
Marcella clambers up the
bedspread and feels her way
along the bed. Then she finds
a gap between their warm bodies.
She pushes and wriggles to make
the gap bigger if there is not
enough room.

Then she cuddles up to Carol and
Ivan. Sometimes she sleeps under
the bedspread, with her paws
tucked under her whiskers. There
she stays, safe and warm, all night.

A photo of Marcella taken by the author.